Loughcrew:

Loughcrew The Cairns

JEAN McMANN

A Guide to an Ancient Irish Landscape

AFTER HOURS BOOKS
Oldcastle

First published in 1993 by
AFTER HOURS BOOKS
Oldcastle, County Meath, Ireland

Distribution: The Gallery Press
Loughcrew, Oldcastle, County Meath
email: gallery@indigo.ie

Reprinted 1994, 1999, 2002
New edition 2005
Reprinted 2010

Series editor and design: Peter Fallon

Text and graphics layout: Elizabeth Macdonald and Emily Payne
Maps: Elizabeth Macdonald
Cairn and site plans: Jean McMann
Drawings of finds: Emily Payne
Carved stones: after Elizabeth Shee Twohig
Other illustrations: from *Discovery of the Tomb of Ollamh Fodhla* by Eugene Conwell (1873)

ISBN 978 0 9521987 0 3

Contents

Acknowledgements

Without the generosity of too many people to name here, this guide could not have been produced. To mention only a few: Peter Fallon provided editing and advice and acted as principal publisher. Emily Payne worked with me on field measurements and plans, and carried out library and museum research. Elizabeth Macdonald brought her skills as a designer to all aspects of the project, including supervising field measurements. Laura Baring-Gould, Laura di Meo, Jean Farrelly, Joe Fenwick, Christie Johnston, Margaret Keane, Juanita Lee, Mandy Loughran, Kyle Schlüter and Mark Stein also provided crucial support in the field and elsewhere. I am particularly grateful to the Oldcastle community, especially the Basil Balfe family, Mary Devin, Jean Fallon, Frank and Rosaline Govern, Ciarán O'Reilly, Phil and Joan O'Reilly, Pauline and Martin Shortt, and Mick, Benny and Nelly Tobin for many kindnesses. Elizabeth Shee Twohig has generously allowed me to draw on her research and base my drawings of motifs on her tracings. I extend my appreciation to the staff of the National Museum both for their expertise and for making artifacts available, in particular Patrick Wallace, Eamon O'Kelly and Margaret Lanin. Thanks are due to Bairbre Ní Fhloinn of the Department of Irish Folklore, University College, Dublin. The following material is reproduced by kind permission of the Head of that Department: Joseph Carroll's stories on pp. 19-20 (Main Manuscript 1160:278-80) and the drawing on p.19 by Eibhlín Ní Sheinchín (Schools' Manuscript 717:6).

Finally, the most crucial support and inspiration for this work came from my husband, Douglas Muir.

Preface

This guide is intended as an introduction to a little-known yet uniquely important landmark, the neolithic cairns at Loughcrew in County Meath, Ireland. The site is a key monument not only in the history of Ireland, but in the world's history of architecture. It lies about two miles east of the north midlands town of Oldcastle, fifty-two miles north-west of Dublin.

To walk the hills of this place is to be surrounded by traces of at least five thousand years of the past. The visitor can explore the extensive, unrestored ruins of one of Ireland's four largest passage tomb cemeteries, and at the same time view a 360° panorama of the Irish countryside. Loughcrew is also rich in the architectural remains of later periods: Iron Age ringforts, medieval crosses and castles, and the sacred and secular buildings of later centuries. This guide is the first twentieth-century publication devoted exclusively to Loughcrew, and includes the first complete plans of the major cairns.

The historical and architectural information in the book provides the reader with factual evidence; I have also included ideas about the use and significance of the site. Spellings are standardised to modern conventions, except when quoting directly. Most important are the maps and plans, designed to help the reader find and identify details of the monuments.

I hope that visitors will think of the cairns not only as beautiful stones in the landscape, but as revolutionary works of art.

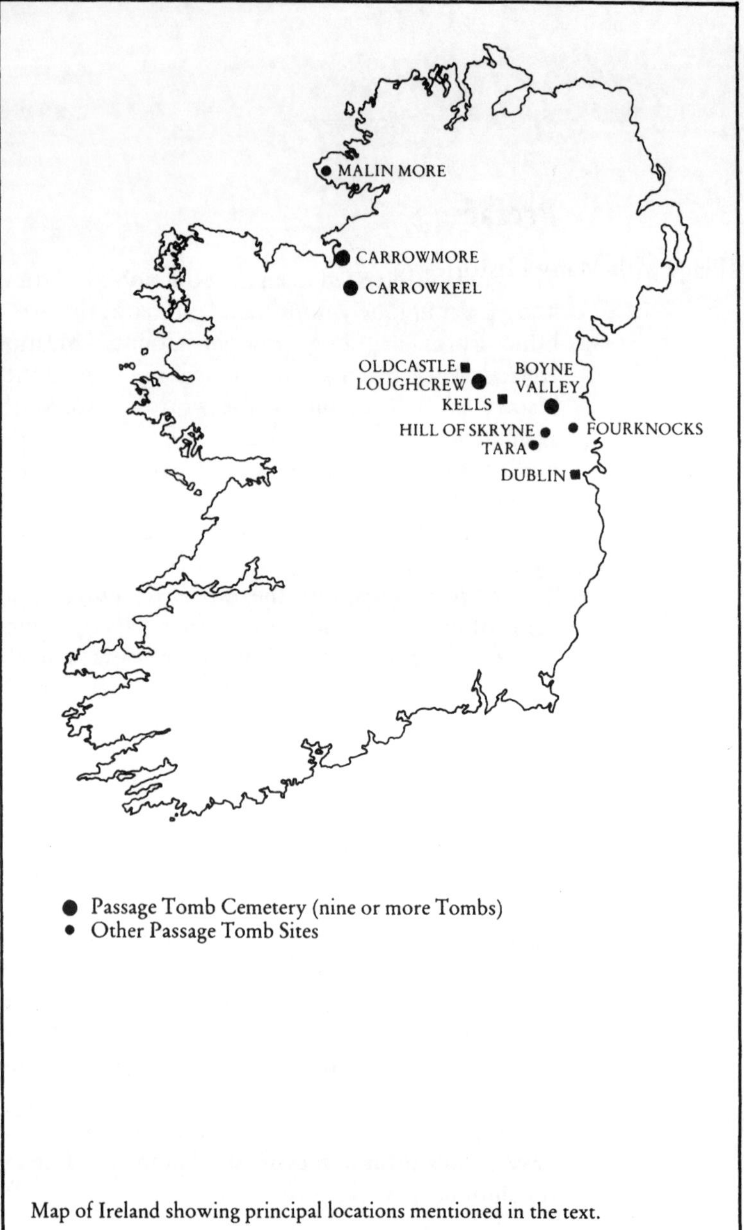

Map of Ireland showing principal locations mentioned in the text.

Introduction

> In the county of Westmeath, in one of the Hills of Loughcrew, which are called by the peasants the Witches Hops, is an extensive excavation, consisting of three large chambers with a narrow passage leading to them. In one of these rooms is a flat altar-stone of considerable size; near to this artificial cave stand two lofty pillar stones known among the people by the names of "the Speaking Stones" and "the Whisperers". Names evidently traditional of there having been oracles or divinations given from these "dark places of the earth".

Antiquarian Louisa Beaufort wrote these words in 1828. Although the "speaking stones" are about four miles to the northwest, the narrow passage she describes must be inside a cairn that stands near the crest of one of the four Loughcrew hills. This heap of rocks (the Irish word *carn* means a heap or pile) can be seen for miles. It is the second largest of the site's thirty or more chambered mounds. These architectural remains are estimated to be approximately five thousand years old, dating to sometime before 3000 BC.

The cairns are what is left of one of Ireland's largest neolithic cemeteries. The name Loughcrew derives from an old townland designation which now includes parts of the hills (see map, pp. 24-25), a small lake, and the remnants of what was once the huge Loughcrew estate, home of the Naper family. John O'Donovan, the nineteenth-century Irish scholar, determined that Loughcrew probably refers to the lake, first called Lough Creeve (*loch na craoibhe*), meaning the lake of the branch, bush or tree. Creeve, he said, described a sacred tree, under whose branches religious rites were held.

Although the archaeological and historical site has long been known as Loughcrew, the ridge is shown on many maps as *Slieve na Calliagh* or *Sliabh na Caillí* which may be translated as the hill of the witch or the hag's mountain. William Petty's map of 1628 shows the hills as "the Calliagh Steppes". A fifteenth century will refers to it as *Trí Choiscéim na Cailligbe*, the three footsteps of the hag, a figure still associated with the place (see *Stories*, p. 19).

Passage Tombs

The remains at Loughcrew are passage tombs, a particular style of neolithic architecture. They have a passage, ordinarily long and narrow, which opens into a domed chamber. They are thought of as tombs because human remains are usually found inside them. Circles, spirals, and other designs were sometimes inscribed on the stones. The passages and chambers were nearly always covered with cairns.

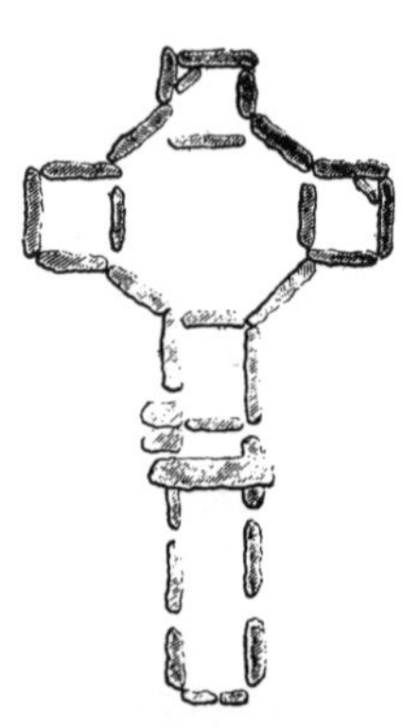
Typical passage tomb plan (Cairn T, by Conwell)

Built with massive boulders called megaliths, Irish neolithic tombs were designed in four main styles: court tombs (a chambered cairn with some type of open court), portal tombs (usually three standing stones supporting a huge capstone), wedge tombs (a rectangular or wedge-shaped chamber, sometimes covered by a cairn), and passage tombs.

Passage tombs occur mostly in the northern half of Ireland. There are only three cemeteries besides Loughcrew with nine or more tombs, all in the north-central area (see map, p. 8). Two of these, Carrowkeel and Carrowmore/Knocknarea, are in County Sligo. The other group is located in the Boyne Valley twenty-five miles east of Loughcrew, and includes three famous passage tombs: Newgrange, Knowth and Dowth.

Newgrange, Knowth, and a number of tombs at Carrowmore have been extensively investigated by modern archaeologists. Although excavation reports have given us invaluable insights into the lives of the people who built and used them, we will never understand exactly the ancient purposes and meanings of any of these sites. Prehistoric societies (that is, early societies without writing) left no histories. At Loughcrew we have neither archaeological excavation reports nor written histories. Still, we can construct a plausible, if speculative, prehistory and history for the place, based on comparisons with similar excavated sites and on the evidence from Loughcrew itself.

This evidence includes not only the mounds and their contents, but an overlay of other remains, both prehistoric and historic, in the Loughcrew area (see map, pp. 24-25). The landscape we see today has been shaped during many periods, ancient and modern. Present-day Loughcrew reflects the influence of Mesolithic, Neolithic, Bronze and Iron Age people (including the Celts), and of Irish pagans and Christians, Norman Catholics, English Protestants, and others. Within the immediate area are ringforts and cashels (earthen and stone enclosures erected by Early Christians), standing stones, stone circles, souterrains (ancient underground passages, often with domed chambers), and what are called *fulachtí fia*, cooking places or pits. Holy wells, stone crosses, and remains of castles nearby date from more recent times.

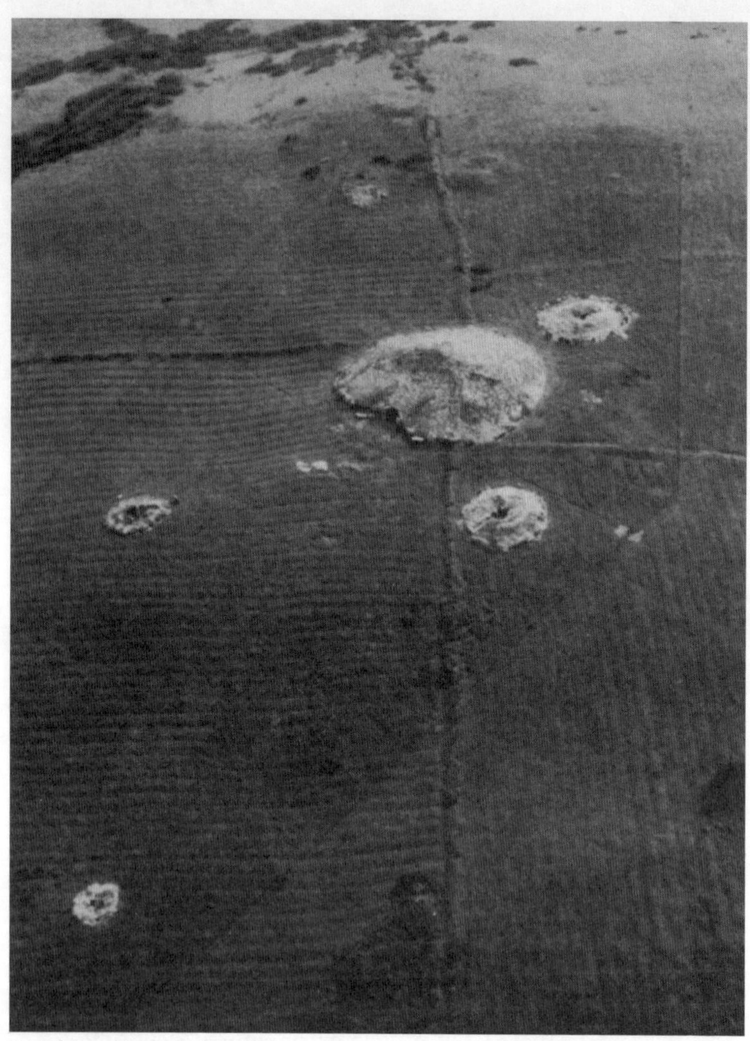

Carnbane East

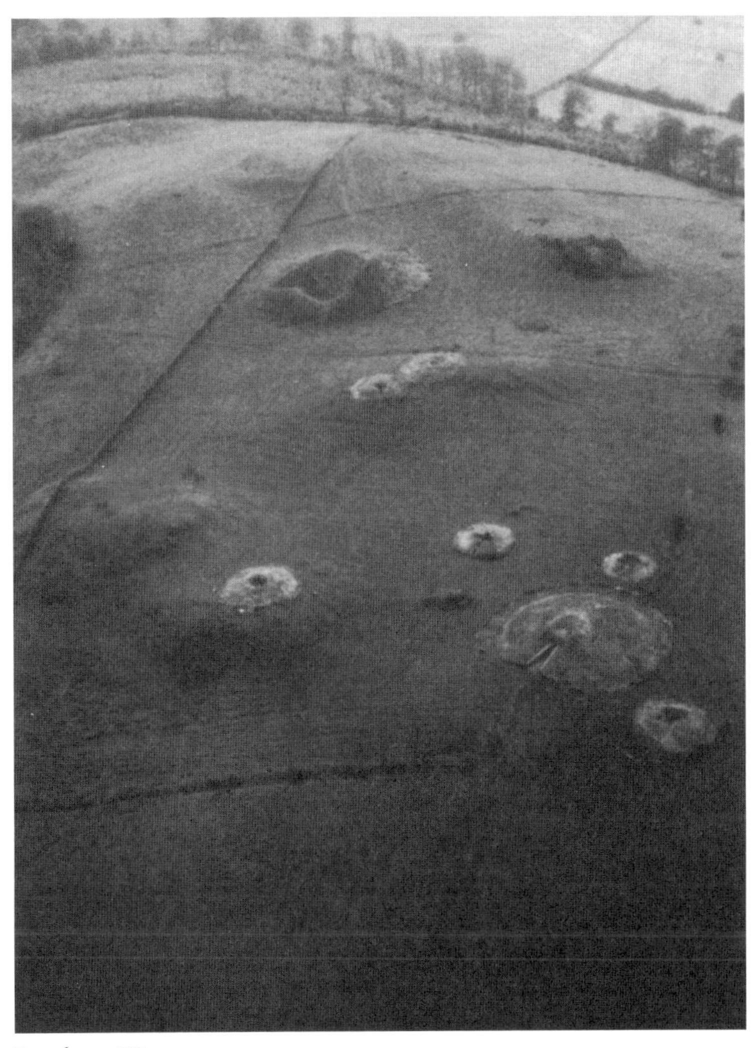

Carnbane West

(Cambridge University Collection of Air Photographs: copyright reserved.)

A Place with Many Histories

ABOVE: Bone flake fragments found by Conwell in Cairn H in 1866

The Neolithic, or "New Stone Age", in Ireland

Perhaps even as early as 4400 BC, people in Ireland began to add farming to their hunting, gathering and herding activities. This could have happened after experienced farmers made the sea crossing to the island from Britain or the European mainland, or as native hunter-gatherers began to experiment with ways to provide additional food. It may have been during a transitional period which included both hunting-gathering and farming that people in Ireland began to build passage tombs.

The world's first stone monuments were passage tombs. The oldest were erected in France and Spain nearly seven thousand years ago, that is, after the cave paintings at Lascaux, but before the Egyptian pyramids. In Ireland reliable dates for the first tombs cluster around 4000 BC. Before that time, at least some groups of people were probably living in the areas surrounding Loughcrew. They may have constructed simple houses and field walls for enclosing livestock, or they may have lived in less permanent dwellings. Evidence of settlements has not yet been found at Loughcrew, although some neolithic domestic structures were excavated at Carrowkeel and the Boyne sites.

Possibly travelling considerable distances in order to participate, neolithic people worked together to build communal tombs in various styles. It is difficult to say how much labour it took to build one of these megalithic monuments; archaeologists' estimates of the work forces range from groups of five people to four hundred. Depending on its size and the number of workers, it might have taken as few as four or more than thirty years to complete a monument. Tombs could have been built in stages, expanded or remodelled over time, or built over previous monuments. Some archaeologists think that the tombs were in use for as brief a period as two hundred years. Many were closed at some point in the past, their entrances securely blocked with stones or rubble.

Although intensive building and other activities took place in Loughcrew between approximately 3500 BC and 3300 BC, there is a puzzling gap in the archaeological evidence both here and in the Boyne Valley during the Bronze Age, from approximately 2500 BC to 500 BC. It is not until the Iron Age that intensive activity seems to have resumed at the Boyne site, and probably at Loughcrew as well.

The Iron Age: approximately 500 BC — AD 500

Although Viking bracelets have been found near Loughcrew, historical documents suggest that the Vikings travelled no further west than Kells. George Eogan's excavations at Knowth show that a group of people settled there and built fortifications during the first few centuries after the birth of Christ. Later this settlement was enlarged and finally Knowth was used as a royal residence. It continued as an important regional centre until around AD 500.

Without further excavation at Loughcrew, we will not know whether a similar overlay of structures and activities occurred there. Objects found in one cairn suggest that the cairn was in use during the Iron Age (see *Archaeology*, p. 18 and Cairn H, p. 36). Early Christian remains, including eleven ringforts and three cashels, indicate that a substantial community had settled near the ridge. The people there probably raised some crops, kept animals, and made metal tools.

The Normans and the English

Loughcrew is still an Anglo-Norman landscape, with its castle ruins and mottes (artificial mounds, sometimes called moats, upon which fortified residences were built). Before Norman times, the O'Reillys probably possessed the site; by the twelfth century it had been granted to the Plunketts as part of the Norman reorganisation of the Kingdom of Meath. At that time, when one Christopher Plunkett owned a castle at or near Loughcrew, areas to the north and west of the site may still have belonged to the O'Reillys. According to the clan's pedigree, an O'Reilly owned Patrickstown and other lands "on the far side of the mountain called Trí Choiscéim na Cailligh e" in the fourteenth century.

During this period native Irish rulers had hopes of expelling the French and English invaders, but they did not succeed. In an order dated July 28, 1653, Colonel James Naper was granted the holdings of the "Irish papist" Christopher Plunkett, including all Sliabh na Caillí except Patrickstown Hill. The Plunketts' most famous son, Oliver, was born in Loughcrew in 1625 and became Archbishop of Armagh and Primate of Ireland. Following false charges of high treason (the "Titus Oates" plot), he was martyred at Tyburn in 1681. Oliver Plunkett was canonised in 1975, the first Irish saint in more than seven hundred years.

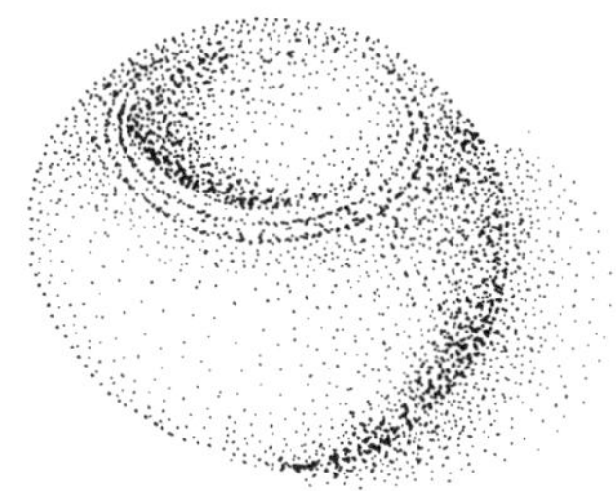

Archaeology at Loughcrew

ABOVE: Stone bowl from Cairn H (5″ diameter)
BELOW: Bone flake found in Cairn H

With the exceptions of Joseph Raftery and Elizabeth Shee Twohig, modern archaeologists have not given Loughcrew much attention. The finds that helped to date Loughcrew and indicate some of the activities that took place there were nearly all obtained by Raftery and an earlier enthusiast, Eugene Conwell.

Eugene Conwell

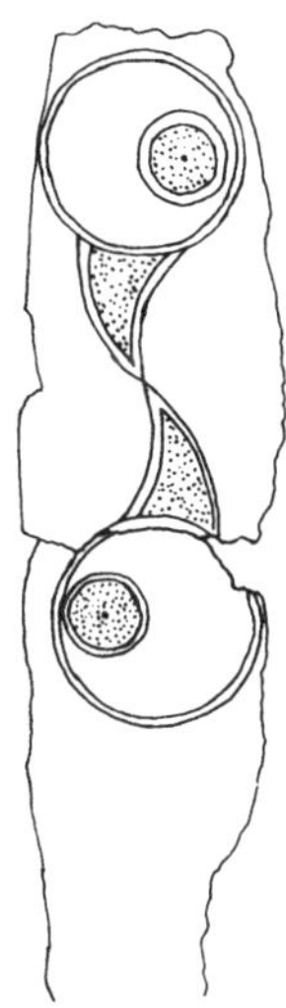

Conwell was the first person to take a serious interest in the monuments at Loughcrew. He lived in Trim and worked as an Inspector of Irish National Schools until his death in 1877. "An intelligent and industrious student" of Irish antiquities (as his obituary noted), Conwell chanced on the mounds in June 1863 when he and Mrs. Conwell had a picnic on one of the hills. Although antiquarian William Wakeman claimed to have reported on them earlier, Conwell considered the site to be his exclusive discovery. He spent weeks searching for traces of cairns, and found the remains of what he counted as thirty-two. He gave these the letter names by which they are still known. All may easily be found today, except for Cairns A2 and E, which are almost imperceptible, and Cairn Z, which is still prominent but has since been identified as a Norman motte (see map, pp. 24-25). In 1864 Conwell read the first of several papers on Loughcrew to the Royal Irish Academy (see p. 21).

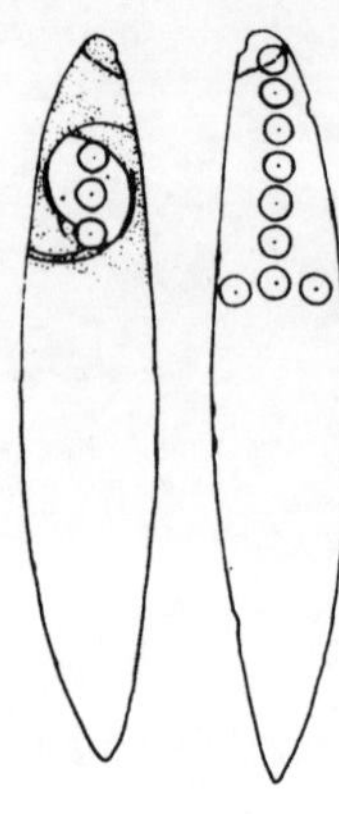

Edward Rotheram

A local landowner called Rotheram from Crossdrum excavated several cairns and the Norman motte below Patrickstown Hill. He reported his finds to the Royal Irish Academy in papers dating from 1877 to 1898.

Joseph Raftery

Raftery was Acting Keeper of Antiquities at the National Museum when he undertook the first official archaeological excavation at Loughcrew in 1943. He confined his investigations to Cairn H, on Carnbane West. Although it resembled a typical neolithic passage tomb, Conwell had found thousands of bone flakes there, some of which were incised with metal tools in a style that dated them to the Iron Age, approximately the first century AD. Because he found some flakes at foundation level, Raftery concluded that Cairn H was built in that age, even though its design appeared to be neolithic. The issue has not been resolved, but Raftery's Iron Age finds suggest that activities took place at Loughcrew some three thousand years after the first cairns were built (see Cairn H, p. 36 and *Interpretations*, p. 42).

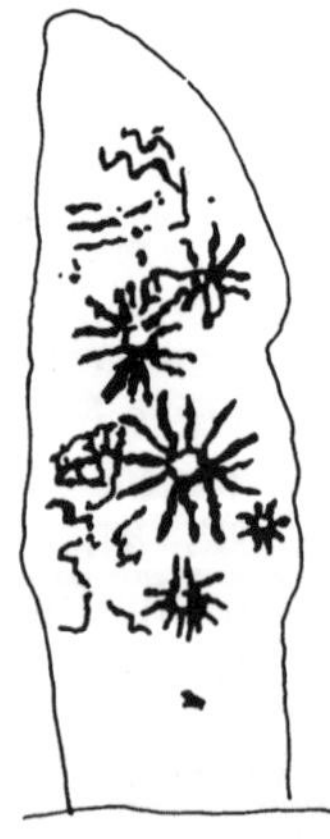

Cairn I R2

Elizabeth Shee Twohig

Shee Twohig, an archaeologist from Cork, was the first to make a comprehensive record of the carvings at the site, although at Conwell's invitation George du Noyer, a noted artist and geologist, had previously drawn a number of the Loughcrew designs. Shee Twohig's documentation is essential for anyone who wishes to study the carvings in depth, particularly since many have deteriorated since she completed her fieldwork in the 1970s.

Stories: A Hag, a Queen, and a King

ABOVE: Drawing by Eibhlín Ní Sheinchín, Loughcrew, 1937

Cailleach Bhéarra

People have probably been telling stories about the Loughcrew hills for more than five thousand years. At present, the legend of the *cailleach* (Irish: a hag or witch) is the best-known tale connected with the cairns. Joseph Carroll, an Oldcastle postman, told these stories about the hag in 1948.

> The "Hag's Chair" is up at the middle hill — Slieve na Caillaigh. It would be roughly three miles from Oldcastle. I know it well . . . The old tradition is that Queen Tailte or Queen Maeve sat in it and proclaimed the laws that were to be observed by the people. There is another old tradition that an old hag called "The Caillaigh Waura" used to sit in it, and it was from that they called it "The Hag's Chair". There's an old rhyme about her:
>
> I'm the Caillaigh Waura:
> I have many changes seen
> I saw old Cairne Bawn a lake,
> But now it's a mountain green.
>
> Another legend about her is that if she'd carry the full of her apron of stones and jump from each of the three hills to the other she'd be mistress over the whole of Ireland. She started from the Cairne Bawn, and when she was jumping she dropped a handful of stones that accumulated to hundreds of tons. She hopped to the next hill, Slieve na Caillaigh, and she dropped another handful of

stones there, and it accumulated into a great cairne. She jumped to the third hill — I forget now what they call it — and threw the remainder of the apron of stones there. And they turned into another great pile, and the three piles of stones are there to the present day. She was going to jump from the last hill to a hill at Patrickstown, and fell and broke her neck.

A pile of stones at the bottom of the eastern slope of Patrickstown Hill was known until recently as the cailleach's grave. This cailleach is famous in Irish folklore. Other storytellers have described her as a superhuman woman who could harvest a field faster than any man, a crone lamenting her youth, a banshee announcing a death, or a Christian nun. She is best known as Cailleach Bhéarra, but has been called by many other names, including not only Waura but Beri, Buí and Vera. She is the subject of the ninth-century lament, "The Old Woman of Beare", and may be a later version of the ancient pagan sovereignty queens whose consent was required for kings to rule. Some scholars think she represented wild nature, as a prehistoric earth goddess.

The following verse about the hag is ascribed to Jonathan Swift, who is said to have collected stories in the area in the early 1700s.

Determined now her tomb to build,
Her ample skirt with stones she filled,
And dropped a heap on Carnmore;
Then stepped one thousand yards, to Loar,
And dropped another goodly heap;
And then with one prodigious leap
Gained Carnbeg; and on its height
Displayed the wonders of her might.

Another of the cailleach's wonders is the Hag's Chair. A massive chair-shaped stone that faces north, it is part of the kerb of Cairn T. Local tradition has it that a wish you make while sitting in it will come true. In other stories, the cailleach sits in this chair to smoke her pipe.

Queen Tailtiu

Several prominent nineteenth-century scholars, including architectural historian James Fergusson and antiquarian George Coffey, thought that Loughcrew was the pagan cemetery of Tailtin mentioned in early Irish epics. Tailtin was renowned as the burial place of the mythical Queen Tailtiu, foster mother of the sun god Lugh. Her cemetery is assumed to be at Teltown, sixteen miles southwest of Loughcrew. However, Queen Tailtiu and Tailtin also have a place in the folklore, if not the history, of Loughcrew.

Ollamh Fodhla

Eugene Conwell, too, thought Loughcrew was once Tailtin. He also proposed that Cairn T, often called the hag's cairn, was the tomb of the legendary king, Ollamh Fodhla ("learned lawgiver"). In fact, Conwell's book on the site, first published in 1872 in the *Proceedings of the Royal Irish Academy*, was titled *Discovery of the Tomb of Ollamh Fodhla*. In the book, he renamed the Hag's Chair "Ollamh Fodhla's Throne".

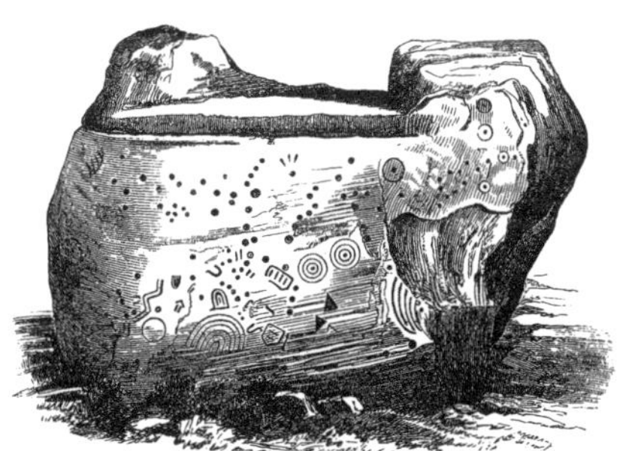

The Hag's Chair (Conwell)

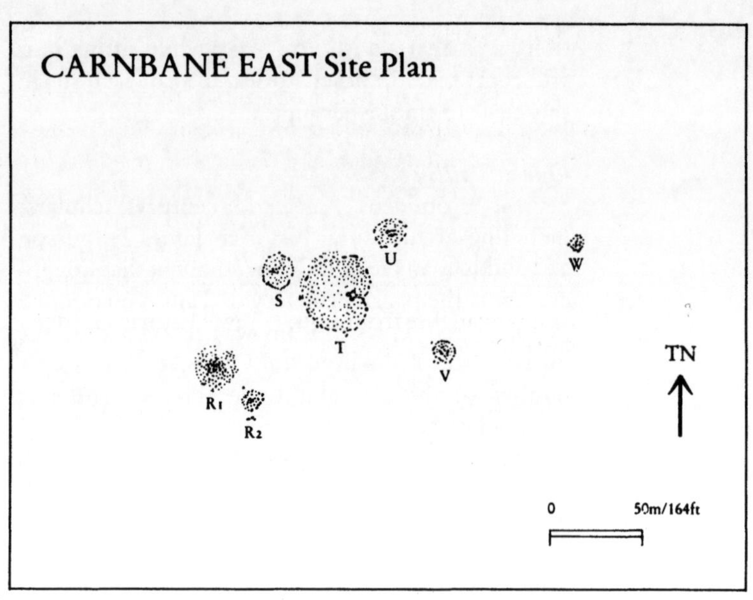
CARNBANE EAST Site Plan
U
W
S
T
TN
V
R1
R2
0
50m/164ft

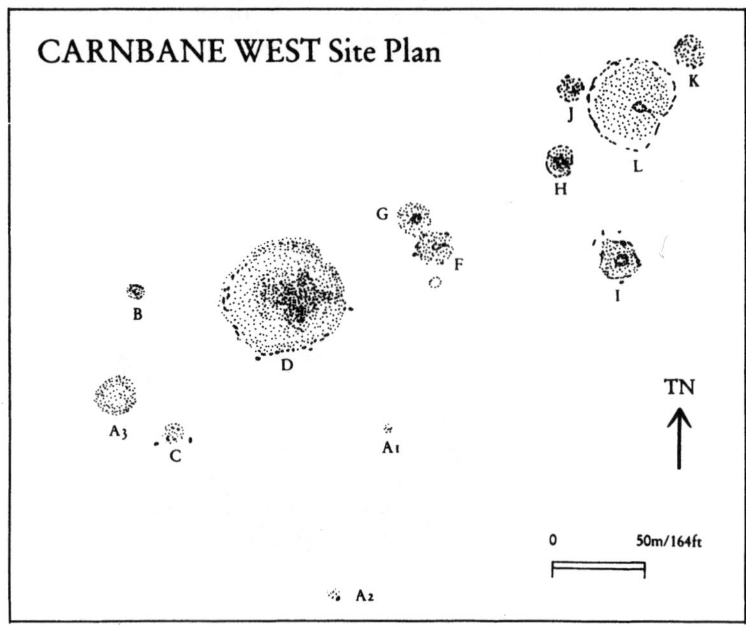
CARNBANE WEST Site Plan
K
J
L
H
G
F
I
B
D
TN
A3
C
A1
0
50m/164ft
A2

The Cairns

From the car park you can walk up to either of the two hills, Carnbane East or Carnbane West, where the most interesting and extensive remains are situated (see site map, pp. 24-25). As you pass through local landowners' fields, please treat their property and livestock with respect. Information about the key for the large cairn on Carnbane East is available from Loughcrew Historic Gardens Coffee Shop (see map) or 049-8541356. You will need a torch to see clearly.

The individual cairn descriptions that follow are not arranged alphabetically, but begin on each hill with the largest cairn and then move around the hill sequentially. Orientations, that is the apparent directions in which the passages face, are given in degrees clockwise from true north (1° to 359°). True north is 0°.

Each cairn description includes a kerb plan (scale: 1 inch = 60 feet). Interior plans (scale: 1 inch = 14 feet) are also included for cairns with relatively well-preserved interior structures. On these interior plans, exceptional carved stones are indicated in solid black, based on Shee Twohig's descriptions and my more recent field observations. In addition, I have followed Shee Twohig's system of numbering carved stones, as C1 etc. for chamber stones, R1 and L1 etc. for righthand and lefthand passage stones.

The stones at Loughcrew are generally described as "limestone", but include, besides calcareous or carboniferous sandstone, a coarse greywacke also called gritstone, and conglomerate. Many were left by glaciers; some are from local outcrops. Chalking or retracing the carvings promotes the deterioration of these ancient, vulnerable surfaces. Please do not mark or damage the stones in any way. Much of the carving visible in Conwell's time has become fainter or disappeared due to weathering; what remains are fragile but significant fragments of human history.

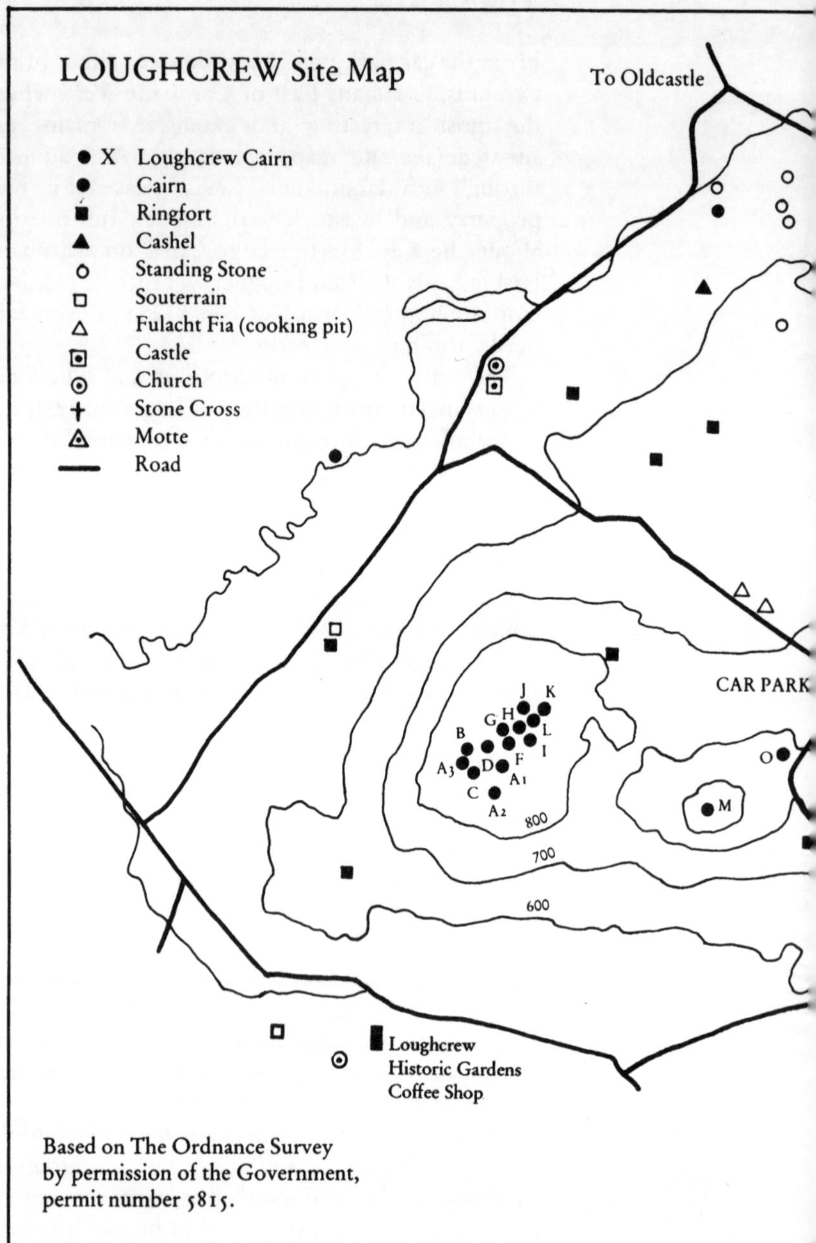
LOUGHCREW Site Map
To Oldcastle
X Loughcrew Cairn
Cairn
Ringfort
Cashel
Standing Stone
Souterrain
Fulacht Fia (cooking pit)
Castle
Church
Stone Cross
Motte
Road
CAR PARK
J
K
G
H
L
B
I
F
A3
D
A1
C
A2
O
M
800
700
600
Loughcrew
Historic Gardens
Coffee Shop
Based on The Ordnance Survey
by permission of the Government,
permit number 5815.

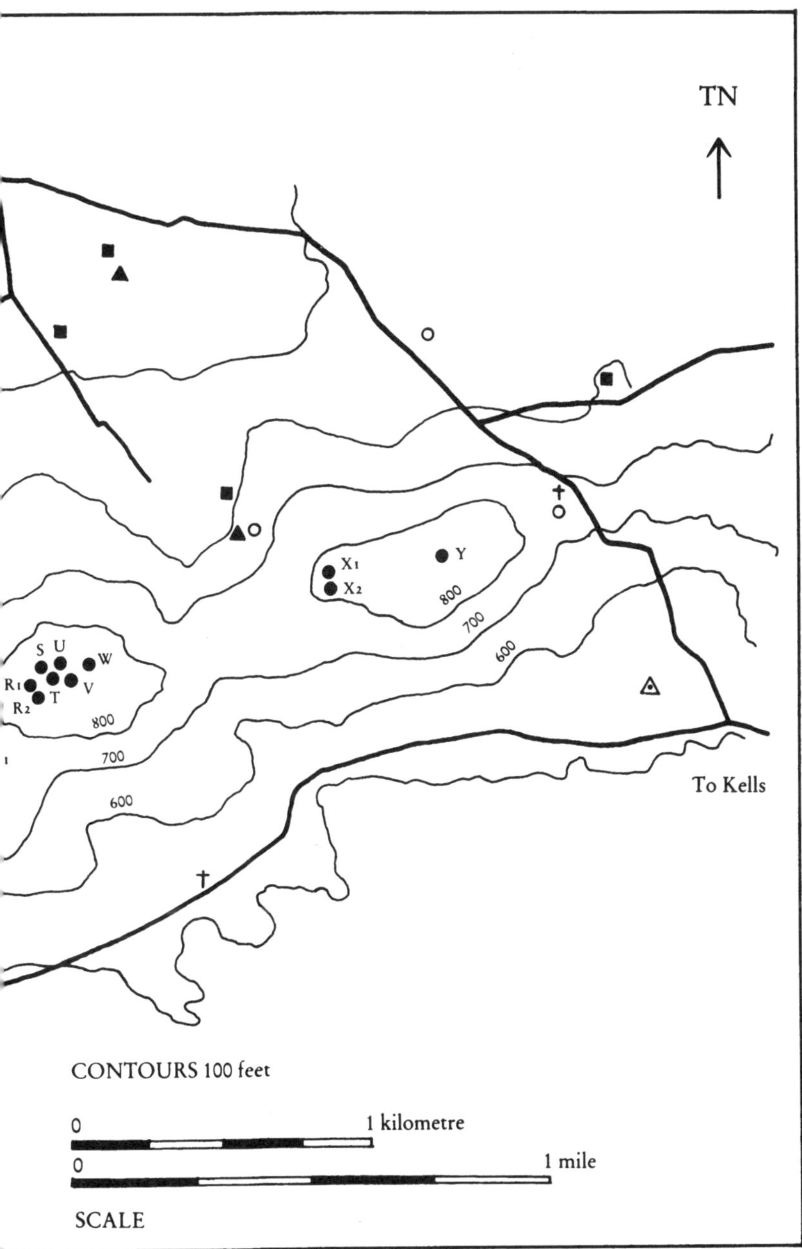

TN
X1
X2
Y
800
700
600
S
U
W
R1
T
V
R2
800
700
600
To Kells
CONTOURS 100 feet
0
1 kilometre
0
1 mile
SCALE

Carnbane East

The path to Carnbane East begins from the car park. At the top of the hill, the large Cairn T (sometimes called "The Hag's Cairn") dominates a group of six smaller, ruined cairns.

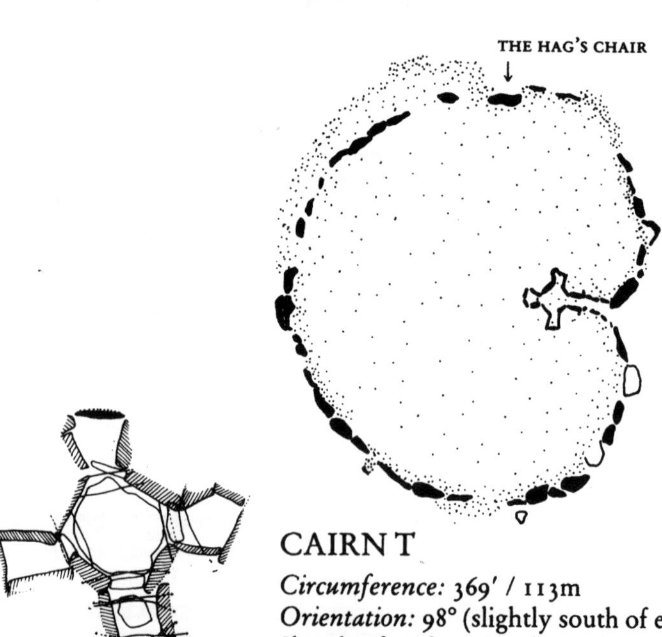

CAIRN T

Circumference: 369′ / 113m
Orientation: 98° (slightly south of east)
Shortly after dawn on the equinoxes, sunlight reaches the cairn interior.
Notable features: The Hag's Chair, the domed chamber and side cells, carved stones.

Exterior

Cairn T is roughly circular, except for the slight flattening and turning in of the kerb at the entrance. Conwell describes a layer of quartz from three to four feet high and two feet thick extending around the cairn behind the kerbstones "as far as was examined". Until a few years ago, large pieces of quartz could be found behind the kerbstones and around the entry. Conwell also reported small lumps of quartz "strewn about" at the base of the Hag's Chair. As the name Carnbane implies (*Carn bán* is Irish for white cairn), at least the most prominent cairns at Loughcrew may have been faced with the white stone. The façade of Newgrange has been restored in this manner; quantities of white quartz were also found at Knowth.

The kerbs of passage tombs seem to have served as retaining walls for the stones of the cairns. Some of the huge kerbstones around Cairn T have fallen forward and a few are missing, but the rhythm of their repeated, massive lengths is still impressive. The largest two flank the entrance to the cairn. The Hag's Chair is the third largest stone in the kerb (see p. 21) and is indented slightly from the perimeter. Faint traces of inscribed designs can still be made out on its surface in good light, along with a cross carved deeply into the seat; in Conwell's time the designs were evidently more visible. Although Conwell suggested that the cross was made by surveyors, others conclude from its style that it was carved in connection with the eighteenth-century practice of holding Masses (officially forbidden) outdoors in secret. In addition to the Hag's Chair, other kerbstones at Loughcrew may once have been carved with designs, as those at Knowth and Newgrange are. These designs may have disappeared as the soft stone at Loughcrew weathered over the centuries.

Interior

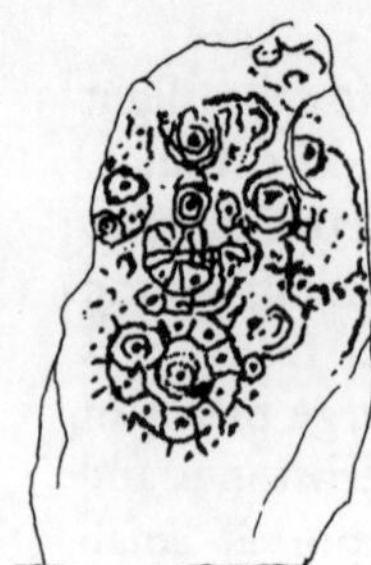

L1

The passage was re-roofed with concrete during conservation efforts by the Office of Public Works (OPW), probably during the 1960s. At the time of Conwell's first visit, only the roof slab over the third pair of upright stones (called orthostats) was still in place. This slab seems to have been removed and replaced nearer the entrance during the reconstruction.

The stone carvings in both passage and chamber are exceptional. On the large pair of stones at either side of the entrance to the chamber there are many worn pits. These may have occurred naturally, but seem to have been deepened artifically. I have discovered that replicas of the chalk and stone balls found in Cairn L fit neatly into many of the pits on these and other stones (see p. 33).

C8

At the end of the long, narrow passage, upon stepping over the high sill, the visitor experiences a dramatic spatial contrast. The domed roof was built by placing the huge, flat stones (called corbels) on top of the vertical stones (the orthostats) that form the chamber walls. Each round of corbels laid horizontally around the perimeter of the chamber was placed a little closer to the centre, so that the diameter of the opening to be covered grew smaller as the sloped roof rose higher. Finally the space left at the top was closed with a huge capstone, and the corbelled roof covered with the stones of the cairn.

Each of the three side cells has a separate, smaller corbelled dome. The carvings on the roofstone of Cell 2 are exceptionally lively and vivid. These extend beneath stones added later, suggesting that this stone, and perhaps others, were carved before being set into place. As you look straight up, you see a modern grate which replaces the capstone which once finished and sealed off the corbelled dome. When he first entered the cairn, Conwell noted that about thirty of the roofing stones were in place "to a height of about ten feet"; the capstone

Roofstone Cell 2

and additional corbels were missing. The OPW has restored the dome to a height of a little over ten feet, somewhat less than its original height.

Under two of the flagstones on the floor of the chamber, Conwell found "fragments of charred bones, small broken stones, and pieces of charcoal". Here are some of his notes:

> The three cists [side cells] were nearly but not entirely filled up with dry, loose stones from the uncovering of the central chamber round which they are placed. The earth on the floor of each was mixed with splinters of burned bones; while in the centre of [Cell 2] a circle of earth, a foot in diameter, inclosed about a hatful of charred bones, which were covered with a flag, above which were raised for about two feet alternate layers of finely broken and larger stones, among which were found some human teeth, and twenty-four bones, here presented, with the ends apparently ornamented with crossed lines. Among the loose stones at the bottom of the central chamber, and close to the entrance of [Cell 3] was found a bronze pin two and a half inches long, with head ornamented, and stem slightly so, and still preserving a beautiful green polish.

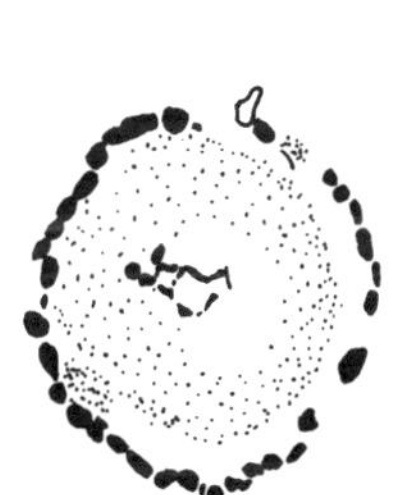

CAIRN S

Circumference: 177' / 54m
Orientation (estimated): 290° (northwest)
Notable features: a kerb of 35 smaller, well-matched boulders.

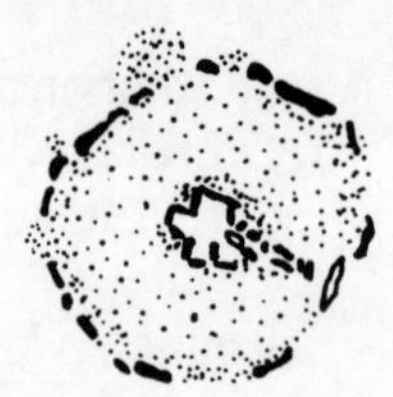

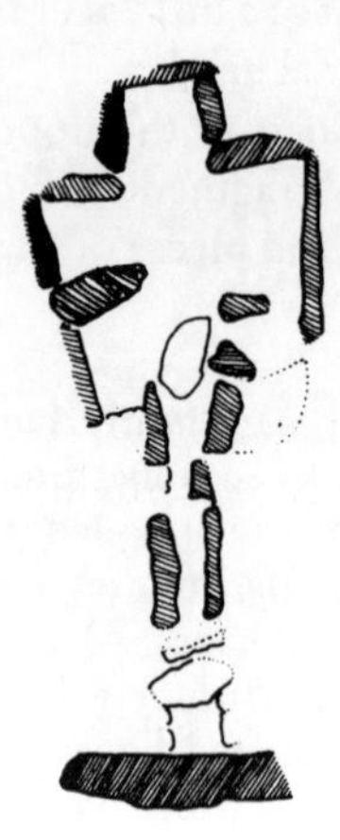

CAIRN U

Circumference: 158′ / 48.2m
Orientation: 108° (southeast)
Notable features: Carvings on all chamber and three passage stones, especially backstones in the side cells; a stalled plan similar to that of Cairn L (p. 33).

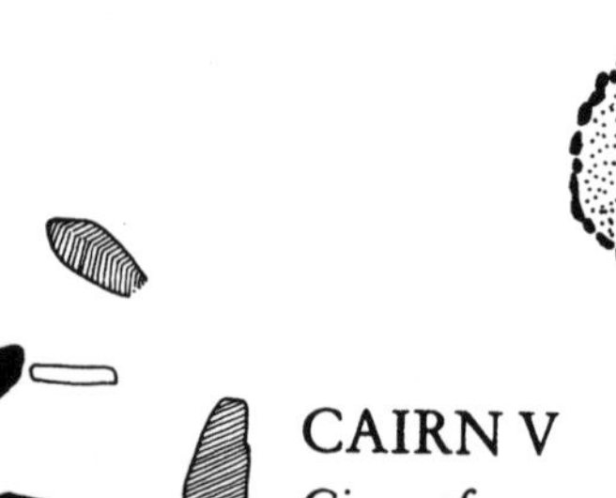

CAIRN V

Circumference: 103′ / 31.5m
Orientation: Possibly 290° (northwest) or 110° (southeast, Conwell's estimate)
Notable features: Nearly complete kerb of 30 stones; carvings on what seem to be chamber stones.

CAIRN W

Circumference: (estimated) 76′ / 23.3m
Orientation: Possibly 168° (slightly east of south)
Notable features: An urn twelve inches high and almost three feet in diameter was found by Conwell in the chamber, beneath a layer of charred bones.

CAIRN R1

Circumference: (estimated): 137′ / 42m
Orientation: 90° (east, Rotheram's estimate)
Notable features: A large stone and tips of three others in the centre of a pit probably left from Rotheram's excavation, which produced "stones of various sizes and one or two pieces of white quartz".

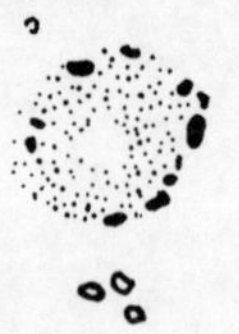

CAIRN R2

Circumference: 72' / 22m
Orientation: undetermined
Notable features: Remains of a kerb (approximately ten stones), and Rotheram's finds: bone pins, stone pendants, fragments of clay vessels, a white flint arrowhead, and a beautifully shaped miniature stone axehead about two inches across.

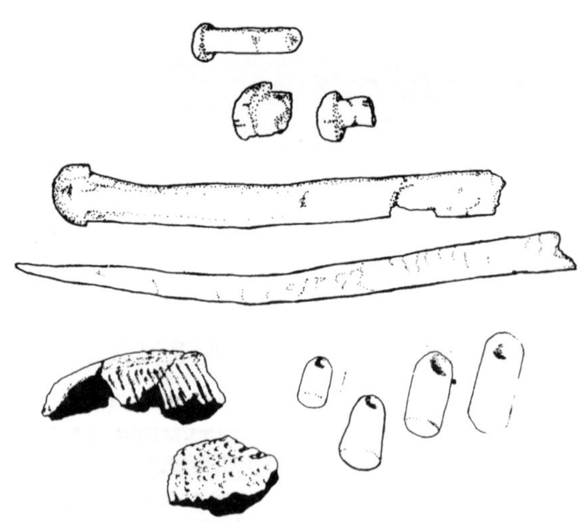

Carnbane West

Carnbane West is reached from a signposted field southwest of the car park. Climb until you reach Cairn L, visible at the crest of the hill. There are two large and ten smaller cairns visible on the summit.

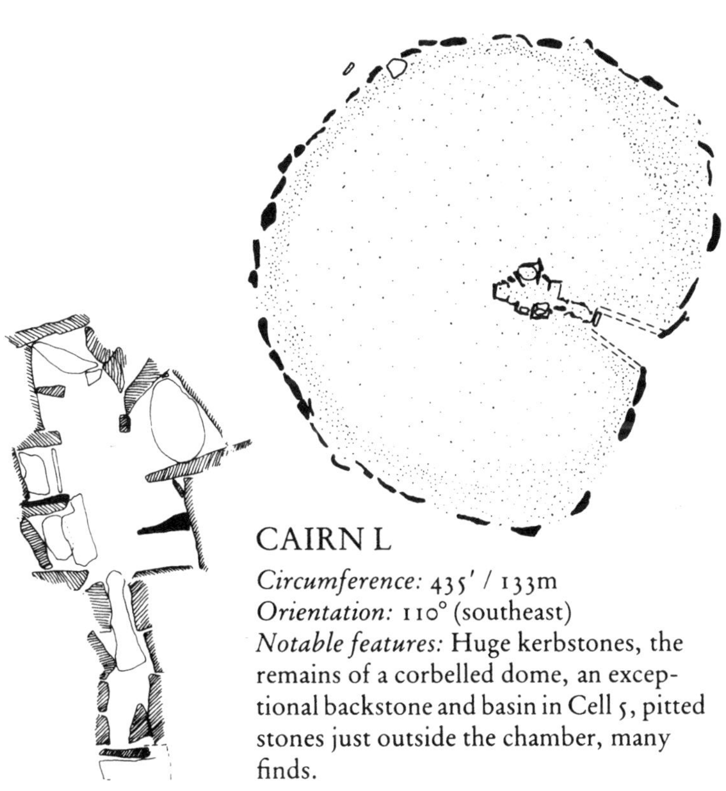

CAIRN L

Circumference: 435' / 133m
Orientation: 110° (southeast)
Notable features: Huge kerbstones, the remains of a corbelled dome, an exceptional backstone and basin in Cell 5, pitted stones just outside the chamber, many finds.

Forty-one huge kerbstones (Conwell found forty-two) now form the perimeter of this mound — some recumbent, but most still standing. Grass may have covered the additional stone. The kerb flattens on each side of the entrance.

The entrance was reconstructed with stone and mortar to a point about halfway down the original passage, probably during the nineteenth or early twentieth century. Orthostat R4 on the plan, like the orthostat outside the chamber entrance in Cairn T, has many pecked and worn depressions. As in Cairn T, replicas of chalk and stone balls (see p. 35) found in the cairn chamber fit into these depressions.

See frontispiece

The corbelled dome of Cairn L probably rose to sixteen feet or more (5 metres) before it was dismantled centuries ago. The concrete ceiling must have been installed at the time other repairs were done, but some original corbelling is still in place. Unlike Cairn T, where three separate side cells extend from the chamber, this cairn has a "stalled" plan. Its seven side cells, designed like stalls, are formed by orthostats beneath one ceiling. As in most Irish passage tombs, the largest cell (Cell 5) is on the right. The basin, the expressive carvings of the backstone, and a slender pillar placed in front of this cell mark it as the dramatic focus of the chamber.

If you look out along the passage of this cairn, a hill to the south, once called Carrigbrack ("speckled rock") or Sliabh Rua ("red hill"), is framed in the doorway. Today you can just make out the place where rubble rises a little, indicating the shape of a cairn that has disappeared.

C3 (east face)

When Conwell first explored Cairn L, many of the huge flagstones that once made up the dome had been removed, and the chamber was filled with loose stones from the cairn. Here is what he found when he examined the area beneath the large stone basin in the north cell:

After the interior chambers had been cleared of all the loose stones, etc., which had filled them up, on Tuesday evening, 19th September, 1865, in presence of Mr. Naper, Mr. Hamilton, Archbishop Errington, and a number of ladies, we turned up this remarkable stone basin, and beneath it were revealed to view several splinters of charred and blackened bones, with about a dozen small pieces of charcoal lying in various directions. On carefully picking the damp stiff earth underneath it, we found imbedded in it upwards of 900 pieces of charred bones; forty-eight human teeth in a very perfect state of preservation; the pointed end of a bone pin . . . a most perfectly rounded syenite ball, still preserving its original polish — nearly two and three-quarter inches in diameter; another perfectly round stone ball, streaked with white and purple layers, and about an inch in diameter; another stone ball, upwards of three-quarters of an inch in diameter, of a brown colour, dashed with dark spots . . . eight white balls [chalk], which had become quite soft; but which gradually dried, on exposure, to a sufficient degree of hardness to enable us to take them away in a tolerable state of preservation.

Chalk balls (Conwell)

CAIRN K

Circumference: 167′ / 51m
Orientation: Possibly 100° (southwest)
Notable features: Siting on a stone outcrop; remaining kerbstones unusually long and thin.

CAIRN J

Circumference: 134′ / 41m
Orientation (estimated): 112° (southeast)
Notable features: Cairns J, K and L have a spatial relationship similar to that of Cairns S, U and T on Carnbane East (see site plans, p.22).

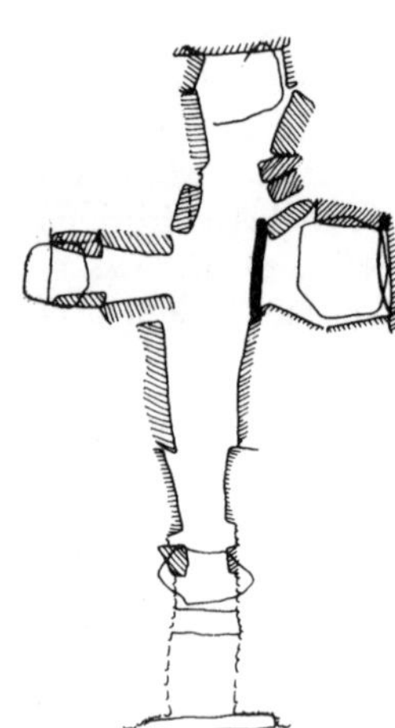

CAIRN H

Circumference: 132′ / 40.5m
Orientation: 111.5° (southeast)
Notable features: Unusual Iron Age finds, including incised bone flakes; a stone basin and strikingly carved sill in Cell 3.

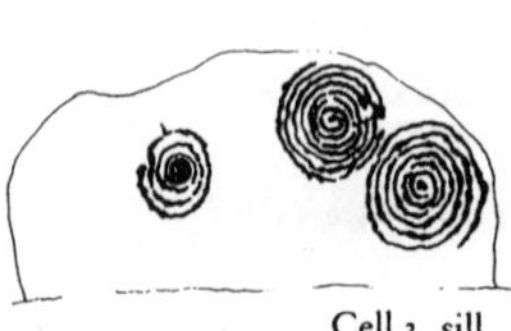

Cell 3, sill

In its cross-shaped design, Cairn H is similar to Cairn T on Carnbane East. Although the kerb was rebuilt after his excavation, Raftery said that he preserved the interior of the cairn as he found it. The style of the carvings on the sill in front of the right-hand cell is somewhat different from the other, more apparently spontaneous designs at Loughcrew. The deliberate rendering of the three concentric rings, and their careful placement near the edge of the stone, seems more typical of later motifs at the Boyne. There are, however, three similar sets of rings on orthostat C3 in Cairn L.

Possible compass leg (Conwell)

Cairn H had been opened and its interior overgrown with grasses long before it was investigated by Conwell in 1865 and 1868 and by Raftery in 1943 (p. 18). When Conwell investigated the cairn, he found the chambers and passage filled with earth and loose stones. Beneath this layer, the passage was "completely packed" with a three-foot layer of burnt bone fragments, along with some small pieces of quartz. In the chambers, as he examined a mixture of broken bones, stones, and earth, Conwell found a small brown stone ball, fire-blackened pottery, pieces of flint, 265 sea shells, "eight varieties of small lustrous or shining stones, a hundred white sea pebbles, and sixty others of different shades of colour".

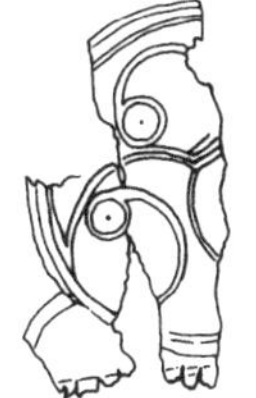

Bone "comb"

Raftery found similar objects typical of neolithic passage tombs. Both also uncovered many finds that were not neolithic: amber and Roman glass beads, bronze rings, and pieces of iron (including what Conwell thought was the leg of a compass). Most interesting of all the finds were thousands of fragments of cowbone which had been shaped into "combs" and "blades". Some had designs incised with metal tools, apparently with the aid of a compass. The style of these designs, along with the presence of glass, bronze, and iron, indicated that the objects were produced in the century before, or the century after, AD 100.

It was the placement of the bone flakes that led Raftery to conclude that Cairn H was built in the Iron Age rather than the Neolithic. His conclusion was questioned by other archaeologists and a complete excavation report was never published, so the issue has not been resolved. What does seem certain is that Cairn H was used for some activities, probably religious ceremonies, during the Iron Age, long after the cairns were constructed at Loughcrew.

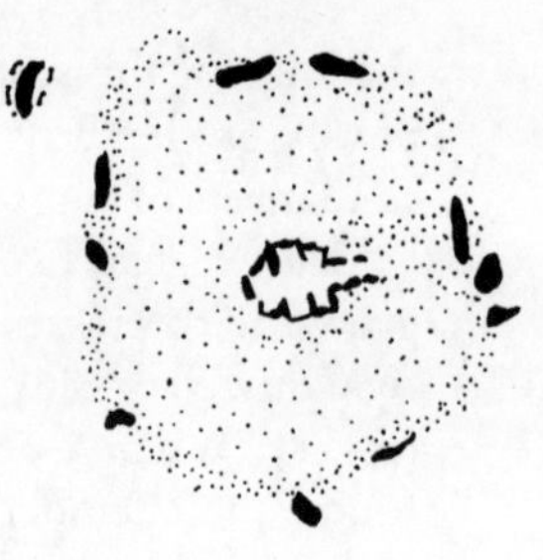

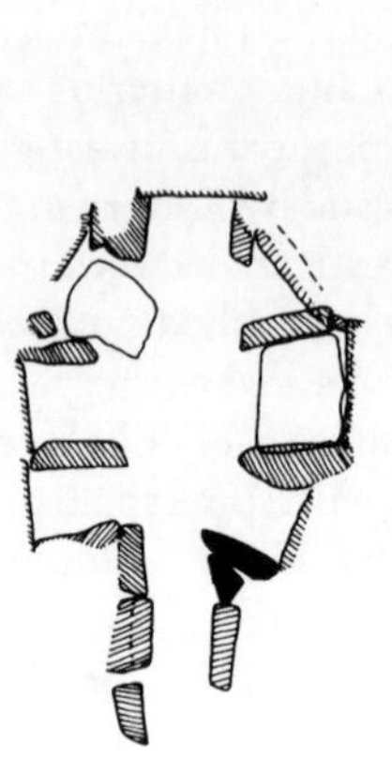

CAIRN I

Circumference: 179′ / 54.7m
Orientation: 80° (northeast)
Notable features: Chamber with seven cells; several strikingly carved stones.

The roof of Cairn I had disappeared when Conwell found it, and its chamber was filled with nettles. Like Cairn L, this cairn has seven compartments. On the floors of five cells, Conwell found square or rectangular flagstones about two inches thick. There were charred bones on four of them. When he lifted these stones, he found more charred bones scattered over a layer of pebbles covering a bed of larger stones. A stone bead and pendant were found beneath one of the flags.

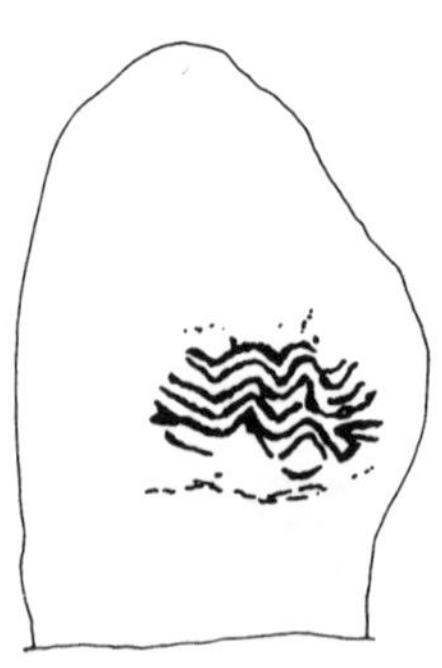

Cairn I C17

Six structural stones in Cairn I are carved, and there are faint stars and zigzags on the flat stone lying in the north cell. Looking eastward from inside the chamber, Cairn T on Carnbane East is framed by the passage. The stone to the left of the passage (C17) is deeply carved with a series of zigzag lines.

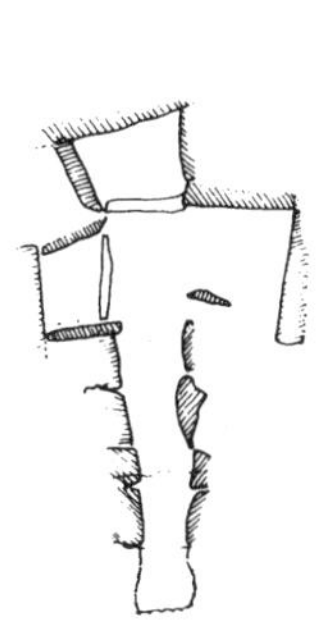
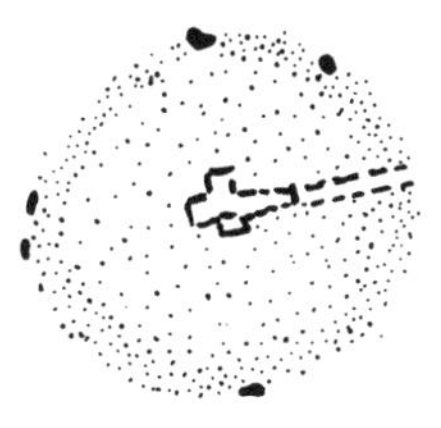

CAIRN F

Circumference: 154′ / 47.1m
Orientation: 80° (northeast)
Notable features: Cross-shaped plan; repeated arcs carved on C1.

CAIRN G

Circumference: 195′ / 59.7m
Orientation: undetermined
Notable features: Kerb flattens as if to avoid Cairn F.

CAIRN B

Circumference (estimated): 74′ / 22.5m
Orientation: 110° (southeast, Conwell's estimate)
Notable features: Three large stones from chamber.

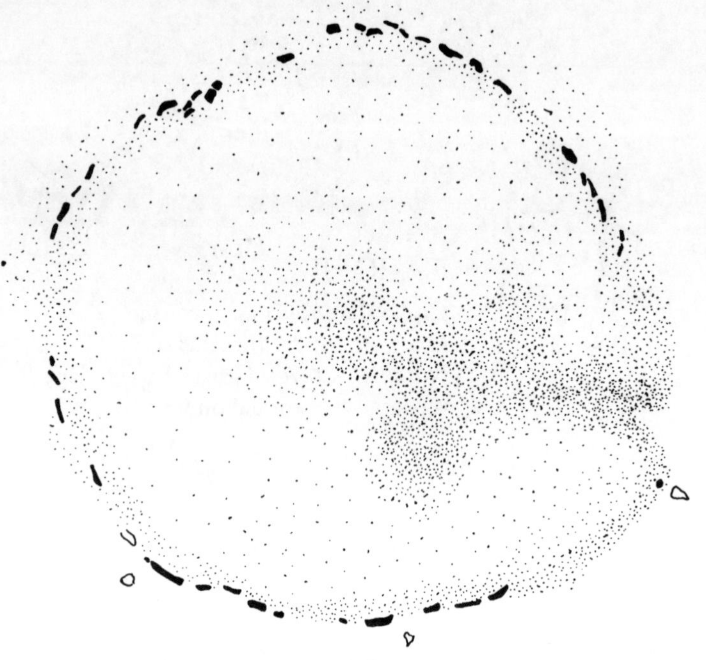

CAIRN D

Circumference: 532′ / 163m
Orientation: Conwell records that the kerb turned inward at a point facing southeast, 110°
Notable features: The largest cairn at the site; no evidence of interior structure.

Cairn D is particularly mysterious. Although it does not seem to have any interior chambers, it had a "perfect" kerb of 54 large flagstones before Conwell investigated it:

> . . . on Monday morning, 4th September, 1865, about a dozen labouring men commenced to remove the stones, and to make a passage inwards from this point . . . . After two weeks spent in this labour, and with as many men as could be conveniently engaged at it, we did not come upon any of the interior chambers; nor have our labours been more successful on 3, 4, 5, 6, 8, 9, and 10 June,

> 1868, when . . . twenty men were busily engaged every day in continuing the transverse cutting through the carn, in search of the interior chambers.

All they unearthed were some animal skulls, teeth, and other animal bones which Conwell thought were from oxen and deer. It has been suggested that this mound is a cenotaph, a monument to someone whose body was not contained within it. Ancient people, one theory suggests, might therefore have left it undisturbed. It could have served as a place of public assembly, as the open space around it suggests (see p. 45). Whatever its ancient use, the ruined cairn stands today much as it did when Conwell abandoned it.

Other Cairns

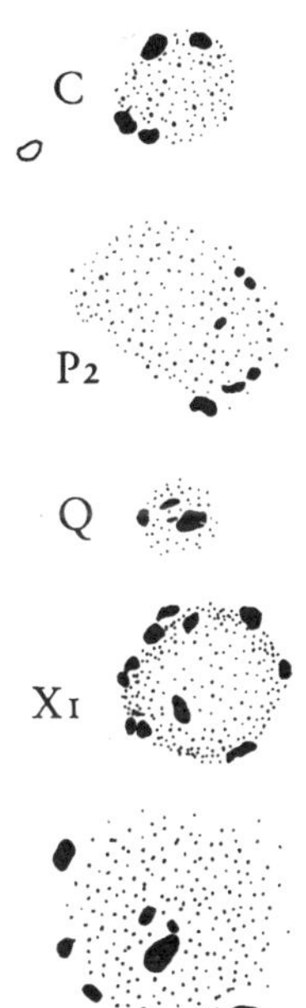

As the site map shows, there are remains of approximately twelve other cairns. A few have several stones standing; the rest are just circular spreads of rubble. Cairn M, on Carrigbrack, is visible as a slightly elevated area at the top. Cairn Y can be detected as a subtle rise in the tips of the pines along the crest of Patrickstown Hill. Cairn N, a third large rubble spread, is on a knoll between Carnbane East and Carrigbrack. On the same ridge, there are a few stones standing from P1 and P2, and none from Q. Cairn O is a low mound near the gate to the field that leads up to Carnbane West. See the site plan of Carnbane East for Cairns A1 (almost no trace left), A2, A3 (in a cluster of trees) and C. Of Cairns X1, X2, and X3, remains of only X1 and X2 can be seen. The central stone of Cairn X1 has a "sundial" design.

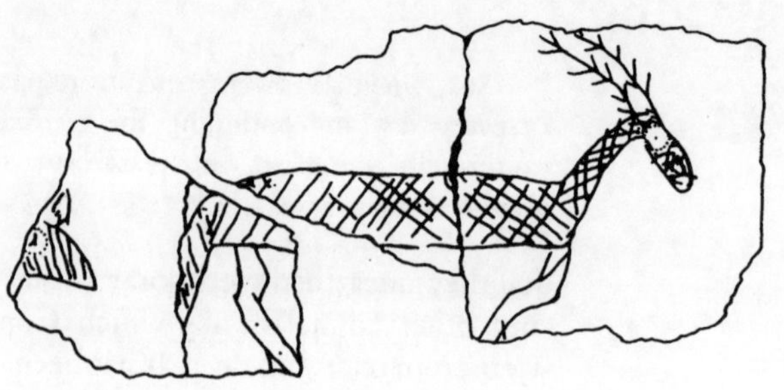

Interpretations and Possibilities

ABOVE RIGHT: Bone flake fragments found by Conwell in Cairn H in 1866
LEFT: Fragment found in Cairn H by Raftery eighty years later

All interpretations, even those of archaeologists, are to some degree subjective. We might say that they are informed guesses. Because our thoughts and perceptions are restricted by the language and customs of our times, it is nearly impossible for us to imagine what might lie outside those limits. And yet, because we possess the physical and mental attributes of ancient people, we may experience similar sensations in this place, as we see the same hills, stones, and sky. Without believing that we can "correctly" picture a past that is forever out of our reach, we can nonetheless feel connected to that past through imagination, informed by our own perceptions and the evidence left to us.

Antiquarians and archaeologists have been making informed guesses about passage tomb architecture for nearly two centuries. At first, they were most interested in the history of culture. They wanted to know, for example, whether the idea for passage tombs came from Asia, or Greece, or Egypt. It was not until radiocarbon dating was perfected in the 1950s that a number of passage tombs were found to be older than Greek and Egyptian stone monuments.

Most scholars agreed that the tombs were used to "house the dead". Many also speculated that the stone carvings and the architecture were designed for sun worship. Both these ideas are credible: human remains were found in the cairns, and the fact that so many of them face eastward indicates that the rising sun was important to their designers. Inspired by the fact that Newgrange is aligned toward the rising sun on the winter solstice, several writers have proposed that the cairns were intended as "observatories", or devices for measuring time. However, none of the tombs at Loughcrew is directed precisely toward an important solar event such as a solstice or equinox, even if we take into account the slightly different positions of the sun in neolithic and modern times.

Many archaeologists would agree that the passage tombs were often oriented toward the sun as part of an acknowledgement of its power. The sun's rays might have been necessary for religious ceremonies, or for blessing certain objects, including relics. The sun has long been worshipped in many cultures, and there are references to its powers in early Irish literature and folk customs. James Martin, a "poor labourer in a mill" who was born and lived near Loughcrew, wrote a verse sometime before 1836 which described the monument as:

> A pagan altar, rear'd by Druids' hands —
> To Bal erected, who, as authors say,
> Was once here worshipp'd as the god of day,
> When superstition held her gloomy throne,
> Before the Gospel in Hibernia shone.

The cairn architecture not only evokes a sun god such as Bal; it may also refer to an ancient earth goddess. As a few archaeologists have suggested, the dead could have been returned to the earth for rebirth. Some of the cairns appear to be oriented towards features of the landscape or monuments which were probably sited with reference to such features. Some face the Boyne Valley site, notably Newgrange; others seem to be directed towards Tara and the Hill of Skryne. A passage tomb at Sliabh Gullion in County Armagh is aligned directly toward Loughcrew.

Passage tombs may have been as much beacons in the landscape as windows to the sky. Some scholars think they served as conspicuous markers defining tribal territories. Many archaeologists have explored the ways in which the tombs might have helped certain groups to remain in power, for example by allowing only elite persons, dead or alive, access to the chambers, or by commemorating certain ancestors so conspicuously.

The cairns might also have been designed to represent different stages of life or death. Cairns have long been known as homes of the *síthe*, or fairy folk. As such they were places of boundary between the worlds of the living and the spirits. In ancient times, their structures could have formed both a bridge and a boundary between the living here on earth and the community's ancestral remains, including their otherworldly spirits.

How the architecture might have been used

What did people do at Loughcrew long ago? How did they use the objects that were found there? Again, we can only guess from the evidence. The artifacts from the site appear more ceremonial than practical. Beads and small axe-shaped stone pendants have patterns of wear showing that they were hung from a string or thong. The bone flakes Conwell and Raftery found in Cairn H were not effective blades. Some have holes perforated at one end and a number are pierced, as though by a needle.

At the time the cairns were in use they must have been profoundly sacred. As the only permanent monuments of the community, they may have served many of the functions we now assign to communal structures. They might not only have contained and commemorated the dead, but also have been the age's equivalent of our libraries, civic centres, theatres, and assembly grounds.

The entire ridge may have been considered

hallowed space, where religious ceremonies were performed both inside and outside the cairns. Certainly at least some people climbed the hills to place offerings and human remains inside and near the mounds. Only a few could have fitted inside, but each of the three largest cairns, D, T, and L, have sufficient space around the kerb for processions. Cairn D in particular seems suited to large assemblies. Perhaps worshippers walked *deiseal*, clockwise or sunwise, around the cairn, as until recently some Irish mourners walked with a corpse around a graveyard. Ancient and modern communities have taken part in processions, dancing, and chanting, and have lit ritual fires to mark important occasions. So we may well imagine that ceremonies took place at Loughcrew, perhaps based on worshipping ancestors *and* natural forces such as earth and sun.

Architectural design

The cairns are characterised by their sharp contrast between interior and exterior design. Outside, they resemble natural additions to the landscape. The smaller ones often take their form from the knolls and hillocks upon which they are situated. Unlike more recent buildings, from temples to skyscrapers, the mounds do not intrude straight lines and strict symmetries into the curves of nature. Their design is more like that of hunter-gatherer sanctuaries, concealed in caves. Yet, unlike the natural spaces of the caves, the interior arrangements of the passage tombs are decidedly artificial. Typically, both passage and chamber, while not exactly symmetrical, are balanced along a central axis. Space is divided into more or less rectangular areas which suggest the cultural notion of differing ranks or social distinctions.

Bone flake

Most recent interpretations of the passage tombs focus on how they reinforce social distinctions and "domesticate" the natural world. However, the design of passage tombs like those at Loughcrew creates a balance between the natural forms of the exterior mounds and the cultural forms of the passages and chambers. Perhaps, in addition to being used in the many ways mentioned above, these first stone monuments served as bridges between nature and culture, as farming began and human relationships to the natural world underwent a revolutionary change. As this change occurred, humans saw themselves less as belonging to nature; rather they saw nature as belonging to them. Perhaps the passage tombs, built during the period when these perceptions were changing, reflected these conflicting views of the world.

The Future

To gaze into the distance from the top of Carnbane East, Conwell claimed, was to see hills in eighteen of the thirty-two counties of Ireland. This landscape has an ancient aspect, with few modern intrusions, although more and more people visit each year. The question of how, and even of whether, such remains should be preserved prompts only difficult and imperfect answers. For many people what gives the site its particular appeal is its freedom from the structures that tourism demands: the wide, well-paved roads, the souvenir stalls, the stairs and footpaths. Because the cairns have undergone so little reconstruction, the experience of the architecture is all the more direct. How to balance essential maintenance and improvements with the beauty of the place as it is today is a crucial issue, to be negotiated with care. Individual, local and national considerations must be taken into account. We hope that those responsible for the decisions experience firsthand the unique power of the place as it is.

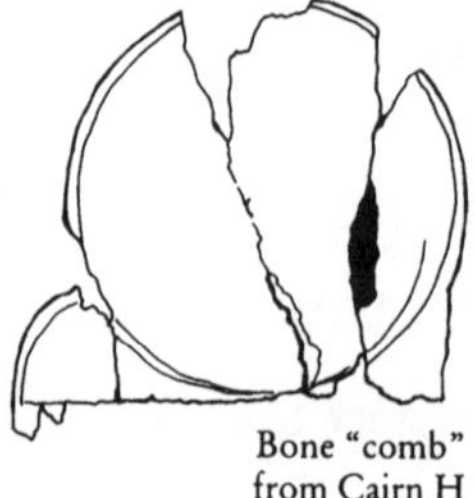

Bone "comb" from Cairn H

Select Bibliography

Beaufort, L. C., 'An essay upon the state of architecture and antiquities, previous to the landing of the Anglo-Normans in Ireland'. *Transactions of the Royal Irish Academy* 15:101-242, 1928.

Eogan, George, *Knowth and the Passage Tombs of Ireland*. London, Thames & Hudson, 1986.

Herity, Michael, *Irish Passage Graves*. Dublin, Irish University Press, 1974.

McMann, Jean, *Riddles of the Stone Age: Rock Carvings of Ancient Europe*. London, Thames & Hudson, 1980.

Form, History and Meaning in an Irish Megalithic Landscape (Ph.D. dissertation) Ann Arbor, Michigan, UMI, 1991.

Moore, Michael J., *Archaeological Inventory of County Meath*. Dublin, The Stationery Office, 1987.

O'Brien, Tim, *Light Years Ago*. Dublin, Black Cat Press, 1992.

Ó Crualaoich, Gearóid, 'Continuity and adaptation in legends of Cailleach Bhéarra'. *Béaloideas* 56:153-178, 1988.

O'Kelly, Michael, *Newgrange: Archaeology, Art and Legend*. London, Thames & Hudson, 1982.

O'Sullivan, Muiris, *Megalithic Art in Ireland*. Dublin, Country House, 1993.

Shee Twohig, Elizabeth, *The Megalithic Art of Western Europe*. Oxford, OUP, 1981.

Irish Megalithic Tombs. Princes Risborough, Buckinghamshire, Shire Publication Ltd., 1990.